Festivals of the World

JAMAICA

Gareth Stevens Publishing
MILWAUKEE

Written by
BOB BARLAS

Edited by
LEELA VENGADASALAM

Designed by
LOO CHUAN MING

Picture research by
SUSAN JANE MANUEL

First published in North America in 1998 by
Gareth Stevens Publishing
1555 North RiverCenter Drive, Suite 201
Milwaukee, Wisconsin 53212 USA

For a free color catalog describing Gareth
Stevens' list of high-quality books and multimedia
programs, call
1-800-542-2595 (USA)
or 1-800-461-9120 (Canada).
Gareth Stevens Publishing's Fax: (414) 225-0377.
See our catalog, too, on the World Wide Web:
http://gsinc.com

© TIMES EDITIONS PTE LTD 1998
Originated and designed by
Times Books International
an imprint of Times Editions Pte Ltd
Times Centre, 1 New Industrial Road
Singapore 536196
E-mail: te@corp.tpl.com.sg
Printed in Singapore

Library of Congress Cataloging-in-Publication Data:
Barlas, Robert.
Jamaica / by Bob Barlas.
p. cm. — (Festivals of the World)
Includes bibliographical references and index.
Summary: Describes how the culture of Jamaica is
reflected in its many festivals, including Reggae
Sunsplash, the Maroon Festival, and the Jonkonnu
ISBN 0-8368-2005-3 (lib. bdg.)
1. Festivals—Jamaica—Juvenile literature. 2
Jamaica—Social life and customs—Juvenile
literature. [1. Festivals—Jamaica. 2. Holidays—
Jamaica. 3. Jamaica—Social life and customs.]
I. Title. II. Series.
GT4827. A2B37 1998
394.26097292—dc21   97-38295

1 2 3 4 5 6 7 8 9 02 01 00 99 98

CONTENTS

It's Festival Time . . .

Do colorful festivals, great music, delicious food, and people dressed to party sound exciting to you? Then, Jamaica's the place to be! Wonder what's Jamaica's contribution to music? Find out at the Reggae Sunsplash. Or you could meet characters with the most unusual names in the Jonkonnu parade. So, gear up for the fun—it's festival time in Jamaica all year long …

WHERE'S JAMAICA?

Jamaica is a little island in the Caribbean Sea. It has a **tropical** climate. This means you can swim in one of its many beautiful beaches at any time of the year. You can also go climbing in the Blue Mountains. Kingston, the capital of Jamaica, is on the southern coast of the island.

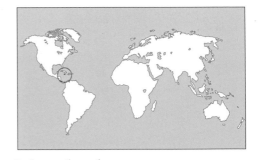

Opposite: A beautiful villa near Ocho Rios, a popular resort on the northern coast of Jamaica.

Who are the Jamaicans?

The first Jamaicans who lived on the island were the Arawaks [ARA-whacks]. They were killed by Spaniards who **colonized** Jamaica in the early 16th century to grow sugarcane. The Spaniards and later the British (who ended Spanish rule in 1655) brought in many Africans to work as slaves on the sugarcane plantations. The Jamaicans of today are mainly the free descendants of these slaves.

Jamaican boys. Most Jamaicans are of African descent.

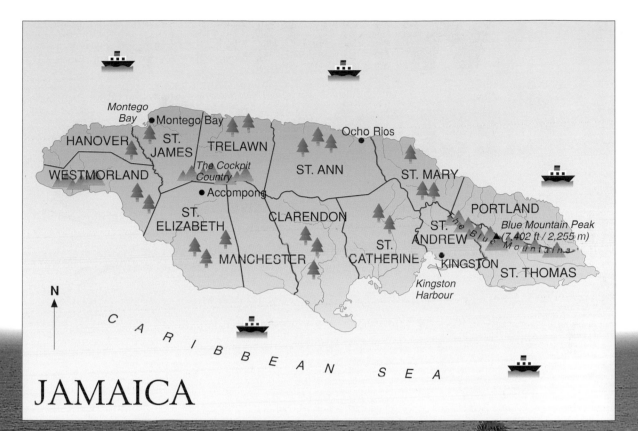

JAMAICA

Montego Bay

• Montego Bay

HANOVER

ST. JAMES

TRELAWN

The Cockpit Country

Ocho Rios

WESTMORLAND

ST. ANN

ST. MARY

• Accompong

ST. ELIZABETH

CLARENDON

PORTLAND

Blue Mountain Peak
(7,402 ft / 2,255 m)

ST. ANDREW

The Blue Mountains

MANCHESTER

ST. CATHERINE

ST. THOMAS

• KINGSTON

Kingston Harbour

N

C A R I B B E A N   S E A

WHEN'S THE CELEBRATION?

Put on your costume and follow me. The fun is just beginning …

Festivals in Jamaica run throughout the calendar year. Each month is filled with many different festivals. So if you are planning to vacation in Jamaica, you are bound to witness one or more of its festivals. Below is a list of some of the popular ones.

SPRING

- ✪ **EASTER REGATTA**—Several boat racing competitions are held in Montego Bay.
- ✪ **KITE FESTIVAL**—Kite competitions, cultural performances, marching bands, circus rides, and other colorful and fun activities are held during this period.
- ✪ **CARNIVAL!**
- ✪ **ANNUAL FLOWER SHOW**
  Manchester holds a grand display of Jamaican plants and flowers every year.

SUMMER

- ✪ **JAMAICA JAZZ FESTIVAL**
  Performers from all over the world gather in Jamaica to play jazz alongside Jamaican jazz artists.
- ✪ **REGGAE SUNSPLASH & BOB MARLEY'S BIRTHDAY BASH**
- ✪ **INDEPENDENCE DAY**

I'm heading for the Kiddies Carnival. Join me on page 25.

AUTUMN

- ✪ **CRICKET SEASON**—Cricketers come together for a month-long series of cricket matches.
- ✪ **JAMES BOND FESTIVAL**
  A week of special events in honor of Ian Fleming, the creator of James Bond.
- ✪ **HARMONY HALL SHOW**
  A celebration of the visual arts and paintings of Jamaica.

Walking on stilts is scary but fun. We are part of the Carnival parade on page 24.

WINTER

- ✪ **JONKONNU**
- ✪ **MAROON FESTIVAL**
- ✪ **NATIONAL PANTOMIME**
  Kingston stages a musical drama full of original songs, dances, and bright costumes for three months beginning in February.

REGGAE SUNSPLASH

Reggae lovers gather in Ocho Rios to celebrate the greatest music festival in the world—Reggae Sunsplash! Reggae, a music with a strong beat, is the favorite music of many Jamaicans. Every year since 1978, top local musicians have been performing to an enthusiastic crowd of reggae diehards that includes Jamaicans and people from abroad. They turn up in big numbers to spend a few glorious days enjoying the music as well as the beauty of Jamaican beaches, and other tourist attractions.

Bob Marley

Bob Marley is a legend in Jamaica. Both the young and old love the music he popularized—reggae. Marley had many talents: he was a singer, guitarist, and songwriter. His songs express a carefree attitude toward life, and many of them are about love. Marley appeared in the second Reggae Sunsplash concert in 1979. He died three years later, but his music lives on and influences pop music to this day.

Left: The statue of Marley in Kingston honors his contribution to music.

Opposite: Marley in concert.

Reggae and calypso

As part of the Reggae Sunsplash celebrations during Bob Marley's birthday bash on February 6th, Jamaican artists sing popular reggae numbers. Fans come by the thousands, drawn to the catchy reggae rhythm played on electric guitars and drums. At this time, too, exhibitions and seminars celebrate Marley's life and works. The eventful week ends with a grand Reggae Sunsplash concert.

Reggae sounds like a mixture of **calypso** [ke-LIP-so] and rap music. Calypso, which is also popular among Jamaicans, is a jazz-influenced musical form that originated in Trinidad, an island in the Caribbean Sea. In Jamaica, there are as many calypso bands as there are reggae bands.

Above: A Reggae Sunsplash participant performs a popular reggae number.

Below: A calypso band. Can you name some of the instruments used?

Above and below: Song, music, and dance are part of every Jamaican festival. In fact, Jamaica has a tradition of storytelling through songs.

Music lovers

Most Jamaicans are brought up to have a strong sense of rhythm. At any music festival, you will see people not only enjoying themselves listening to the music, but also taking part by clapping their hands, singing along, or even breaking into a dance!

Think about this

Do you know that the song "Wonderful World (Beautiful People)" was sung by a Jamaican reggae artist named Jimmy Cliff? What is your favorite music? How is it different from reggae?

11

JONKONNU

T he Jonkonnu [JOHN-con-ooh] takes place around Christmas time in Jamaica, especially in the small towns and villages. Jamaicans spring-clean their houses and prepare for a big family celebration.

Masked and costumed performers

No one knows for certain how the festival got its unusual name. Many people think that it came from *gens inconnu*, which is French for "unknown people." If true, this is indeed a good name for this festival because everybody in the Jonkonnu parade wears colorful masks and costumes. The masks represent special characters, such as Cow Head, Horse Head, Jack-in-the-Green, Policeman, King, and Queen. A favorite character in the parade is the Pitchy-Patchy Man. His costume is made from strips of different colored cloth sewn together. As he dances, the strips sway from side to side.

Performers in the Jonkonnu parade wear masks so nobody knows who they really are.

The parade

On the day of the parade, Jamaicans dressed in colorful costumes make their way through the town, singing and dancing. They are accompanied by musicians who play the **fife**, a small flute. Other musical instruments, such as wooden or steel drums, are also used.

The parade stops in front of some houses, where the characters perform for the people there. The drummers display their drumming skills, especially if the householder gives them some **rum** to drink. This performance is called a "break out." When the parade resumes its journey, spectators join in behind the performers and dance along to the music.

At last, the parade reaches a big open area. Here, people either join in the singing and dancing or just watch the fun. When it ends, everyone goes home for a big meal. If you were there, someone might give you a **"sno-cone"** made of ice and flavored syrup!

In the Jonkonnu parade, the dancers and musicians are just inches away from the spectators.

13

Guessing games

The Jonkonnu parade is not very common now in the big cities of Jamaica, but Jamaicans living in villages and small towns still enjoy it. Part of the fun during the Jonkonnu is in trying to guess who the masked characters really are. For all you know, the Pitchy-Patchy Man may be your uncle or teacher out to have a good time! Wouldn't it be fun to dress up as Jack- or Jill-in-the-Green and fool everyone?

Above: A boy sips a cola drink to beat the heat during the celebration.

Opposite: The colorful strips of cloth and the face mask set the Pitchy-Patchy Man apart from the other performers.

Left: A performer with a tall, elaborate headdress and a face mask succeeds in hiding his identity.

Think about this

Many of the characters in the Jonkonnu parade wear masks to hide their real identity. Have you ever worn a mask? Are there any celebrations in your country where people wear masks?

THE MAROON FESTIVAL

Many of the slaves brought in by the Spaniards to work on the sugar plantations ran away to live in the hills. The Spaniards called these runaway slaves *Cimarrón* [see-ma-RON], and over time the word was shortened to Maroons. The Maroons of today are the descendants of these runaway slaves. Their home is called "The Cockpit Country" because of the many small hollows in the hills.

Special heroes

The Maroon Festival takes place every January in Accompong. It was here that Cudjoe, one of the leaders of the runaway slaves, held meetings with his people. He and a female leader called Nanny are looked upon as special heroes. The Maroons still elect their own leader.

Performers at the Maroon Festival dress differently from those at the Jonkonnu parade. Their outfits are not as colorful, and sometimes their faces are smeared with ash.

16

On the plaque:

KOJO OR CUDJOE IS REGARDED AS ONE OF THE GREA
RESISTANCE LEADERS AGAINST THE MILITARY-PLANTATION
GOVERNMENTS HI H F LLOWED THE NC H CONQUEST OF 1655
THIS TOWN OF ACCOMP NG GREW OUT A FORTIFIED MAROON
OUTPOST ESTABLISHED ABOUT THE COMMENCEMENT OF THE 18TH
CENTURY DURING THE FIRST MAROON WAR. THE TOWN WAS
ESTABLISHED BY ACCOMPONG AT THE DIRECTION OF HIS
BROTHER KOJO. THE WAR CONTINUED FOR NEARLY 50 YEARS.
FINALLY THE ENGLISH ASKED FOR PEACE. ON MARCH 1, 1739,
A TREATY WAS SIGNED, BRINGIN THE FIRST MAROON WAR TO AN
END KOJO DIED AT OVER 80.
JAMAICA NATIONAL TRUST COMMISSION

Celebrating escape from slavery

People travel all the way from Kingston to the hills to be part of the Maroon Festival. During the festival, performers sing the ancient songs of their people while beating traditional drums. They also perform dances that have been handed down to them through the centuries by their **ancestors**. Many of the songs are about the brave things that Cudjoe and Nanny did to protect their people. The songs also celebrate the Maroons' escape from their brutal slave masters.

Above: On Cudjoe Day, the Maroons gather in Accompong, one of the most important Maroon villages in The Cockpit Country. Celebrations are held to mark the peace treaty that was signed with the British.

Right: A procession in the town of Accompong is part of the Maroon Festival celebrations.

17

Traditional instruments

As in any other Jamaican festival, the music in the Maroon Festival has a clear African beat to it. The rhythm is very strong. Drums are the main instruments used in this festival. A special musical instrument called the **abeng** [a–beng], a horn, is also played.

The big feast

After the dancing, the whole community sits down to a big feast. This is prepared in open pits over wood fires by the best cooks in town. The favorite foods are curried goat and spicy pork.

Above: The abeng is played during the procession.

Opposite: Performers and spectators come together to enjoy a day of remembrance of their past.

Right: These women will sit down to a good meal after the dancing. In the old days, Jamaicans ate wild pigs and sometimes cooked iguana lizards.

Think about this
The Maroon Festival features a unique musical instrument, the abeng. Are there any musical instruments that are found only in your country? How are they played?

INDEPENDENCE DAY

Independence Day is held in August each year. It celebrates the independence of Jamaica from the British in 1962. Another special day is National Emancipation Day, which celebrates the official **abolition** of slavery by the British in 1838. These two days are often celebrated together.

Above: Children rehearsing for Independence Day not only have fun but also learn about their cultural heritage.

Below: Jamaican men and women display their amazing drumming skills.

A festival for all

Independence Day is probably the most colorful and exciting festival in Jamaica. Children in schools all over the island prepare special songs, dances, and plays for this day. Like every festival in Jamaica, Independence Day celebrations feature different kinds of music and dancing. There are also parades and award ceremonies for people who have done good deeds during the year. There is even a national song contest to select the best Jamaican song of the year.

Dancers in the parade at the packed stadium are cheered on by the spectators.

Young girls in pretty costumes execute special steps for a dance. Preparations for the performance start early in the year.

Biggest celebration in Kingston

Independence Day celebrations are held in towns and cities all over Jamaica, but the grandest one takes place in Kingston. In the morning, there are speeches and award ceremonies, and sometimes a special flag-raising ceremony. Then comes the event that everyone waits eagerly for—a parade of gaily decorated **floats** in the green, black, and gold colors of Jamaica. In the afternoon, everyone comes out to the biggest open space in town to watch dances and other performances. The children play special games called "ring games," which always take place in a circle. These games have specific actions and are often played to songs. Both grown-ups and children like to dance around a **maypole** set up on the performance ground.

Think about this
When is your country's National Day? Are the celebrations similar to those in Jamaica? In what ways are they different?

Left: Soldiers stand at attention during the national day guard-of-honor inspection.

Below: These young girls are part of a series of performances that take place before Independence Day on the first Monday of August.

Special food

At the end of Independence Day, there is always lots to eat! Special food is prepared for this occasion. Entire families sit down to a big meal of fish or curried goat eaten with peas and rice. Afterward, there will be fruit, such as mangoes and soursop. Children may even be treated to sno-cones. As for the adults, there will be plenty of their favorite rum to drink. Music and dancing continue late into the night.

23

CARNIVAL!

The Jamaican Carnival is a week-long festival that takes place just before the religious season called Lent. It is celebrated in Kingston, Montego Bay, and Ocho Rios with parades, parties, and other events. Like the Jonkonnu Festival, the main events take place in the streets, some of which are closed to traffic during this time.

Feathers, paper, cloth, and paint—anything and everything goes into making a Carnival costume.

Dressed to party

The Carnival parade features colorful floats. Walking alongside these floats are the performers—jugglers, acrobats, singers, dancers, clowns, and others, all dressed in fanciful costumes. These costumes are one of the main attractions of the Carnival. Jamaicans give them funny names, such as "Sunshine City" or "Check-it-out." Many of the people who come to watch the parade are also dressed up.

Dancing

At the end of the parade, everyone begins dancing. A popular music that Jamaicans like to dance to is the *soca* [SO-ka], which has a strong rhythm. Calypso and reggae are also played.

24

Other Carnival activities

Besides the street parade and dancing, there are also music and storytelling competitions. There is even a special "Kiddies Carnival" that children attend in fancy dress. This is their chance to take part in games and competitions and walk away with prizes.

Left: Clever puppet masters move gigantic puppets that seem to float in the air.

Above: A female performer wears an eye-catching costume and a unique headdress.

THINGS FOR YOU TO DO

A great many percussion instruments are used in Jamaican music. One of them is the *maracas* [ma-RA-kes].

What are maracas?

Maracas have a hollow case filled with seeds or beads. When you shake them, they make a rattling sound. If you follow the steps below, you can make this instrument yourself.

How to make maracas

Get two small, empty plastic bottles of the same size; for example, soda or water bottles. Using permanent markers or poster paints, decorate the bottles with different colors. Fill a quarter of each bottle with green or red beans. You can also fill the bottles with buttons or beads from discarded clothes or jewelry. Seal the bottles with their caps. Congratulations! You are now the proud owner of your very own maracas!

Sing to the beat of the maracas

Try shaking the maracas while singing the song below. Ask someone to play the piano while you play the maracas. Have fun!

WATER COME A ME EYE

Things to look for in your library

Another Kind of Music. (film).
Caribbean Islands Handbook. Sarah Cameron (Passport Books, 1997).
Cultures of the World: Jamaica. (Times Editions, 1994).
http://www.jamaica-gleaner.com (website address).
Jamaica. Simon Scoones (Wayland, 1992).
Jamaica, A Visitor's Guide. Harry S. Pariser (Hunter, 1993).
Jamaica Handbook. (Moon Publications, 1993).

MAKE A PITCHY-PATCHY MAN

I n the festival of Jonkonnu, many participants wear brightly colored costumes. The Pitchy-Patchy Man wears one of the brightest costumes. Follow the instructions below carefully, and you can be a Pitchy-Patchy Man yourself!

You will need:
1. A cardboard box
2. Scissors
3. Xacto knife
4. String
5. Pieces of old fabric
6. Glue

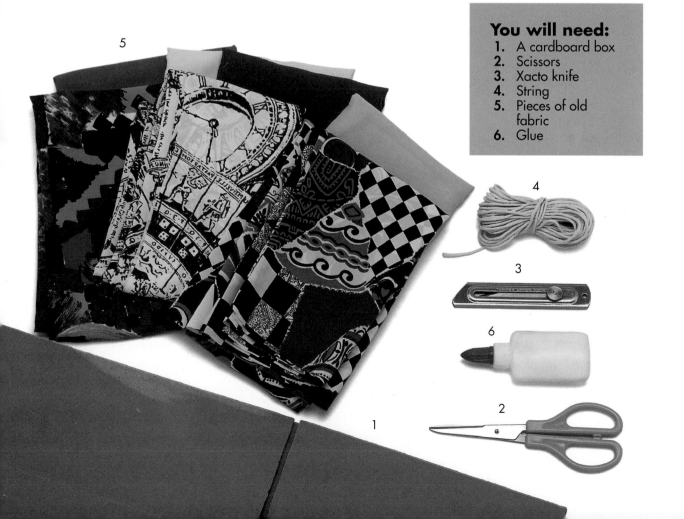

1 Look for a cardboard box that fits around the middle section of your body. Cut out the top and bottom flaps of the box.

2 Punch four holes on the top part of the box—two in the front, and two at the back.

3 Thread two strings, 24 inches (60 cm) long, through the holes at the back and at the front, one on each side.

4 Cut the pieces of old fabric that you have collected into long strips. Glue the strips one by one onto the top of the box.

Step into the box now and fasten the strings around your shoulders. You can also make a hat to go with your costume, or simply paint your face!

MAKE A PINEAPPLE FOOL

A fool is a dessert made of fruit, sugar, cream, and sometimes eggs. Here's a really yummy pineapple fool that is simple to make. You can also use fruit like raspberries instead of pineapples.

You will need:
1. A knife
2. A pineapple
3. A board
4. A sifter
5. A whisk
6. ¾ cup (180 ml) cream
7. 2–3 tablespoons sugar
8. A bowl
9. Measuring spoons
10. ½ teaspoon vanilla extract
11. A wooden spoon

1 Have an adult help you cut a fresh pineapple into small cubes. Put the cubes in a sifter to drain for at least ten minutes.

2 Whip the cream in a bowl until it is stiff enough to hold its shape. Add sugar to the cream. Pour in the vanilla extract. Mix well.

3 Chill the whipped cream and pineapple cubes separately in the refrigerator. Just before serving, add the cubes to the cream and blend them together.

4 Spoon your fool into individual bowls or sundae glasses. Serve right away!

GLOSSARY

abeng, 19	A horn-like instrument played during the Maroon Festival.
abolition, 20	A formal end to a practice, for example, slavery.
ancestors, 17	People related to you who lived a long time ago.
calypso, 10	A jazz-influenced musical form that is popular in the Caribbean.
colonize, 4	Establish a settlement.
fife, 13	A small flute made of bamboo.
floats, 22	Vehicles in a festival procession that carry displays and people in costumes.
maypole, 22	A tall decorated pole around which people dance.
Reggae, 8	A popular music with a strong regular beat.
rum, 13	An alcoholic drink made from the juice of sugarcane.
sno-cone, 13	A dessert made of ice and flavored syrup.
tropical, 4	Very hot and wet weather.

INDEX